Under The Watchful Eye

To Helen Southoff,
Thanks for your
nice comments on my
poetry. May 1996
be good to you
E. Deahl

James

Poetry by James Deahl

In The Lost Horn's Call   1982
Steel Valley   1984
No Cold Ash   1984
Blue Ridge   1985
Into This Dark Earth   1985
A Stand Of Jackpine   1987
Geschriebene Bilder   1990
Opening The Stone Heart   1992
Heartland   1993
Even This Land Was Born Of Light   1993
Tasting The Winter Grapes   1995

Prose by James Deahl

Real Poetry   1981
The Future of Poetry: Despair or Joy?   1991
The Andromeda Factor   1991
INNER[ENTER]TEXT   forthcoming from Broken Jaw

Edited by James Deahl

The Uncollected Acorn   1987
I Shout Love and Other Poems   1987
The Northern Red Oak   1987
Hundred Proof Earth   1988
Let the Earth Take Note   1994

Under The Watchful Eye

Poetry and Discourse

by James Deahl

Broken Jaw Press
Fredericton • Canada

Under The Watchful Eye
Copyright © 1995 by James Deahl

Acknowledgements:
All of the poems in this book have been previously
published. The author wishes to thank the editors of the
following periodicals and book publishers for their
interest in his work: *Anthos, Envoi* (Wales), *iota*
(England), *Laurel Review* (USA), *Mainichi Daily News*
(Japan), *Poetry Toronto*, Aureole Point Press, Envoi Poets
Publications (Wales), M + N Boesche Verlag (Germany),
Moonstone Press, and Unfinished Monument Press.

Published by Broken Jaw Press.
Cover art by Dan Bridy.
Cover design by Joe Blades.
Author photo by David Allen Greene.
Book design by Gilda Mekler.

First edition
Printed and Bound in Canada
10 9 8 7 6 5 4 3 2 1

Canadian Cataloguing in Publication Data
James Deahl, 1945–

Under the watchful eye

ISBN 0-921411-30-8

1. Title.

PS8557.E223U63 1995   C811'.54   C95-950117–7
PR9199.3.D37U63 1995

Broken Jaw Press
M•A•P•Productions
Box 596, Station A
Fredericton NB E3B 5A6
Canada

A Note of Thanks

The author wishes to express his gratitude to Joy Katz, Terry Barker, Judith Stuart, Michael Wurster, Jennifer Footman, and Gilda Mekler for their help with his manuscript. This book, whatever its strengths and flaws, is much better as a result of their advice and encouragement.

For my father,
Henry Vance Deahl

and for
Justus and Wilma Deahl,
who always made their home at Hiorra
my home,

this book
and my love.

My earliest memories are of Ulysses and mounds of dead Jews. Ulysses was my paternal grandfather, and when I knew him he resided at a rest home down by the Black Fork River in the isolated hill town of Parsons, West Virginia, surrounded then, as it is today, by abandoned mining camps and the half-overgrown welts of their waste tips. He was, in those days, moving steadily towards the close of his life, suffering a bit from black-lung, the result of years of working deep underground wrapped in the eternal, bituminous night.

The Jews were victims of Nazi racism, and I saw their gaunt bodies year after numbing year at the Rivoli Theatre in East Pittsburgh. As far back as I recall, I would walk with my band of friends from Forest Hills through the slow, yellowbrick afternoon quiet to the Rivoli for Saturday matinees. Although the fighting was over, the owner of this moviehouse would show old World War II newsreels. These often focused on the Nazi death camps. When Germany fell, these massive extermination centres were liberated. Allied troops, with the international media in tow, entered the camps and the full horror of Hitler's final solution was revealed. This was the start of the great labour of documenting the gravest evil of our time, and some of these films and still photographs ended up on movie screens around the world. These images, presented to us in stark black-and-white, were too terrible to describe, too terrible to even think about, and yet, far too terrible to ever forget — a legacy of stacked and broken corpses starved beyond understanding, the memento mori of a savage business.

I have no idea why the owner of the Rivoli showed these newsreels during children's matinees, nor do I know how they affected others. Perhaps he wanted to instil in our young minds the horror and tragedy of racism and anti-Semitism. If this was his goal, he attained it in my case.

But the effect of these old, yet still vivid, newsreels was broader than this. They also showed the destruction of war in general. We saw the bombed cathedrals; we saw the corpse-strewn fields; we saw the flattened villages. We learned that our generation must put an end to war. Hollywood movies might try to depict warfare as a glorious adventure filled with strong, unwavering heroes and beautiful, adoring young women, but the newsreels of World War II put the lie to that. We children were shown what an actual war was like, and I grew into manhood hating war, racism, and violence.

These early childhood memories perhaps had something to do with my opposition to the American invasion of Vietnam, which started in December of 1961 when President Kennedy sent the first armed helicopters, backed by a force of 3,200 U.S. soldiers, to that poor, war-ravaged nation. By the summer of 1965, tens of thousands of ground combat troops were pouring into Vietnam and I had become involved in the anti-war movement. This was during my student days at Electronic Institutes, and the peace movement was still unpopular. It seems I had learned much from those old newsreels.

From Ulysses I also learned much. Grandfather Deahl was a man who laboured hard all his life. (And those were the days when hard work was really hard.) When he died at the age of eighty-three he wore the marks of the Depression and tough times on his face. As one might imagine, life in the coalfields of Appalachia was not easy in the best of times, and Ulysses did not live there in the best of times.

In addition to his job in the local mine, Ulysses operated a 42-acre farm. This farm was back in a hollow where the rocky slopes were so steep that only mules or stout horses could work the land; it was a farm that could never be mechanized. Like many other mountain families at the turn of the century, the Deahls tried to be as self-sufficient as possible. Money was in short supply and the mine paid in scrip, not cash. Ulysses and his growing family needed the farm; there was work for all, children as well as adults.

Husk

After the first hard frost
farmers enter upon their frozen land
to bring in the year's feed corn.
Along rough county roads

draught horses plunge in heavy air,
forged shoes striking congealed ruts.

Stalks rustle in the wind's teeth
brittle with the scent of snow.

Through the long dusk the grain
is dragged by solitary workmen
to barns that lean red
into the blood of a harvest sky.

All autumn the men go
silent among the ragged trees that
mark off field from hand-worked field.
Stiff with sleep they dream of corn,

dream of that bullet of frost
lodged in the heart of every kernel,
of the dead weight of each iron
ear in the shucking hands.

Yet, after working all those years in the mine, keeping the family farm, fathering eight children and sending most of his sons to college, he had little to show for it but poverty and poor health. This was the sad end of most men who had been involved in the mines, and it did not really matter if they had been labouring men or supervisors. The wealth they created left the hill country, never to return.

(Having been raised in a working-class family in western Pennsylvania and West Virginia, I did not need to study Marx or Lenin to understand the nature of social injustice. Much later I actually did read my Marx, with a helping of Lenin on the side, but they have had little to do with my current

4

ideas. My father put in almost forty-six years at Westinghouse Electric, so I reached adulthood with a pretty sound understanding of the Pittsburgh version of industrial capitalism, its good points as well as its bad.)

Grandfather's children would have kept him in style, but he was certainly not about to accept their "charity". To my young eyes, he was a gaunt, frail, white-haired widower who had clearly suffered from mining in the days when ponies and mules were more valuable to the operators than men.

Like grandfather, my uncles and aunts are, in general, proud, taciturn, and extremely religious. They are German-American Protestants with a streak of Calvinism running bone-deep. Stern would be the word that comes most readily to mind: one sat in church and did not move an inch during even the longest sermons.

And still, there were happy days. Family reunions, church socials, and cakewalks abounded, as did picnics and swimming parties down by the Possum Hollow dam. It was here, at Possum Hollow, that my father, Henry Vance Deahl, received his first, and only, swimming lesson. Dad was the youngest of five boys and was therefore the last to learn how to swim. The lesson was straightforward . . . his brothers took him out in a rowboat and, in the middle of the lake, tossed him over.

To this day its dark, cool waters remain a fine spot to swim.

Possum Hollow

for Henry Vance Deahl (1904 - 1993)

Thick stone
dressed and set tight where twin hills draw near,
huge blocks slicked green with moss in flower.

Behind the dam the lake runs dark
under ash and broad-crowned maple

a twisted vein of obsidian,
deep and shallow turnings.
Fish sink from sight in long cool currents.

Thirty years ago the family on the town side
kept the cleanest garden

now the apple tree grows large,
unpruned.

Coal mines shut,
no work but for logging and that not steady.
Young people drift

leave for Morgantown,
Clarksburg,
                or the tired mill towns of Pennsylvania.

Possum Hollow beneath a late spring sky
that first hint of dryness at the back of the wind

Route 92
winding the gap in Chestnut Ridge
south to the Tygart.

To journey from Pittsburgh to Hiorra in the days before interstates, one would take Pa. Route 51 south to Uniontown. This road led right through the heart of Fayette County and the rich coalfields of southwestern Pennsylvania; tipples and beehive ovens, interspersed as they were with corn fields and hillside pastures, would swing into view at almost every turn as the state road followed the land's dips and folds.

At Uniontown one could take U.S. 119 into Morgantown. From there it was W.Va. Route 7, past the stark, white-shrouded trees surrounding the limestone works at Greer, over to Reedsville and W.Va. Route 92 south to the gap in Chestnut Ridge. This was at Newburg, the nearest village to Hiorra. As an adult I would learn that Newburg was the site of the first of numerous West Virginian coalfield disasters. Thirty-nine miners died there on January 21, 1886 and, although Ulysses was just seventeen years old, he heard of it. It could hardly have been otherwise since he had all his life lived deep in the Preston County coal country.

Indeed, it must have already been clear to him that he would soon have to enter the mines. To make money at all one looked to mining or the coke ovens; there was virtually nothing else. And either would kill you if you stayed with it long enough; it all depended whether you wished to die from black-lung or acid-lung.

A man had to be both tough and lucky to survive his working years. Ulysses did.

Beehive Ruins

Hard by green blazed road
mouths of the hills' flung limbs engulf fern
and the daring crow
with their hot red cup of charred firebrick.

This bright sumac noon
a flowering blackberry twists through
blue spiderwort leaves
under the serpent voice of the sun.

And the song of sun
in the fanged skysail lifts mist and crow
from scarred valley bed
into the dreams of the town's lost men.

From their coke-black stones
grey rakers watch a barked locust root
strangle its searing
heart in the hole at the earth's red thigh.

My parents and I would visit West Virginia several
times each year and, although the drive south
would occur during the daytime, our trip back to
Pittsburgh would most often take place after
nightfall. I especially liked to watch the rows of
glowing beehives, fire shooting small spikes of
light from their charge holes, as they lit night and
silent, swaying trees. To me they were witch-fires,
mystery fires flowing with the curves of the hills.
They called to me in darkness.

I loved them as I loved the steel mills, especially
the Bessemer converters and open-hearths, and I

was lucky to catch the tail end of this era. When I was employed at the Edgar Thomson Works of United States Steel it was almost a century old, having been opened in 1873, and the open-hearth process was still used, although the converters were things of the past. At some point between my boyhood in Forest Hills and my adulthood as a steelworker in Braddock, those glorious, flaming converters had been absorbed into the grey history of industrial technology. I've always regretted their loss, and clearly recall that orange sky at night when the fires of Braddock flooded the heavens for miles around.

And in my memory Pittsburgh is like that, a circle of light and dark, each flowing into the other in a continuous, pulsing flux. Viewed from a distance the mills and coke batteries were vivid with light; flametower and stack tip, they filled my valley with their radiant strength. But on the inside, within the caverns of iron and steel where men laboured their youth away, a darkness lived like the cunning heart of a beast, hungry and restless.

Then, too, there was the great dichotomy of city and country; it provided a background to my every experience. On one hand, I was fascinated by the steel mills that lined the Mon valley and longed to work within their gates. On the other hand, I was swept away by the rugged beauty of Hiorra, with its deeply shadowed hollows and dense hardwood forests. The underground mining and coke industry was already dead at Hiorra when I began visiting my ancestral home. Thus, the rows of burning beehive ovens were things I would meet on my way south to the pastoral stillness of Ulysses' house, where the distant sound of the bell around a dairy cow's neck would awaken me on high summer mornings, when by breakfast the season's thick heat had already entered that cup of forest where the Deahl homestead stood shaded by its single hemlock and a towering tuliptree.

It was here I could lose myself within the folds where mountains had clashed when the earth was still young. Chestnut Ridge and Irish Ridge set boundaries for a world of whisky and revivalists, of hidden creeks that never saw a flicker of sunlight and of the spreading scars of strip mines that laid the earth bare to the hot, blue sky.

Bit by bit, I began to learn the history of this place . . . the natural as well as the human history. The latter was, of course, the history of my people, one of the founding families of Preston County. In many ways the Deahl tribe was typical of Appalachian hill families; they saw generations of struggle in pioneer conditions. My great-great-great-grandfather Henry fought in the Revolutionary War, and the Deahls were well established in West Virginia when it was still the far western frontier of the plantation state of Virginia, with very few roads (if one could call those rough tracks "roads") and no railroads or canals. It was damned hard to even get to the area until the Civil War.

Eventually, my family would produce men like my cousin, Dr. Jasper Newton Deahl, who founded the College of Education at West Virginia University and would later serve as its first dean emeritus.

Hiorra

Beehive oven bones
rust in this orange soil —
        western flank of Allegheny Range
        buckling against southern tip
        of Laurel Mountains down from Pennsylvania

layers of rock cut at angles
shale and good thick coal,
        fossil leaves and roots
all covered
rounded green with trees.

Hiorra:
        hundred foot tuliptrees in spring bloom
wind and sun alternate
along the length of the valley

in scrub sumac
the last of the tipple —
fallen timbers
        grey on top where hot sun strikes
        thick moss alive with scarlet flowers.

And the suffering.
No sign marks this place
or tells the story
        of days when mines burst

with the sound of ponies
or the valley opened
brilliant with flames.

A brassiere hangs discarded
in blueberries;
        the cicadas are a dazzle of mating.
Full wilderness returns,
south of the road
the ovens lie choked with roots
        all but three buried entirely

on the north side
brick arches slip and crack
        exposed to wind
        most half gone.

Hundreds died in the days
between Harrison and Hoover

        most died old,
        some when the earth
        settled too fast

and scores of rakers died
faces black with coughing,
lungs torn by acid-riddled air.

The mines shut down forty years ago,
yet this May the creek
still orange with sweat.

As a boy in a 1950 Ford
I remember the chestnuts

trips to Preston County
        the bare crowns white and high,
        silver above the shorter, living trees.

Father watched them go
slipping away one by one,
        "a disease of the bark"

today, the tulips remain
just as tall
            but slimmer
            more restrained
        their great yellow-orange flowers
        drifting down into thick crests
        of black oak and gum.

West Virginia rising, falling
in the sun's steady heat

black holes left by beehive wombs,
a lament of coke
underfoot

                        zones of silence
                        then the cicadas start

                        all at once.

They came for the coal
and took what was easy to get

        villages sprout
then disappear into leaves

wives   families
lovers tangled under wild grape
or naked in mossbank by Raccoon Creek

the old men gaunt on porches
lame and coughing;
all those years
        seven Republicans in Washington
            — fools pursuing Whitman's dream.

Houses grew along the valley flowing with fire,
the ebb and thrust of dull red
        on a night sky of clouds
and the children watch
garlands of flame:
        a lifetime passing on the road
        to Tunnelton.

Chant of the hills, that B & O Road.
Beehive coke for
Pittsburgh,
        fuel for foundries
        in Wheeling and Youngstown.
Slow twisting coal trains
down the dark rails

long metal snake
　　under the watchful eye of a
　　　sun-flashed hawk
　　circling in August heat.

Hauling away the mountains.

Steel for the world,
money for fine-turned houses on Fifth Avenue
far from the breath of ovens
　　working day and night.

Whole hillsides of crab apple, chokecherry
　　collapse
slide into creeks

mud killing the fish
for thirty miles.

Coal and coke,
　　vast river of night
where the earth comes crashing through.

Our dead lie here
orange in the ground

their bones call out
　　from every ridge,
relate their story

the day-by-day courage
of work.

Ultimately, the Baltimore and Ohio Railroad would be driven up the mountain valleys and through Hiorra. Still, when my great-grandfather, George Washington Deahl, returned from service with the Union Forces during the Civil War, the population in the area drained by the Cheat River was only about six people per square mile.

Travelling through this part of the Appalachians one reaches the crest of a mountain to see nothing at all made by human hands. Such scattered villages as exist cling to rivers and creeks in the narrow bottomlands. The steep ridges — some once cleared and farmed, others still virgin — are covered over by chestnut oak, wild cherry, pignut hickory, and the endless, unstoppable web of grapevines pulling the trees to their death. It's a lonely, insular land of a few, struggling settlements, separated one from another by miles of tangled, rocky hills.

Even today a strange remoteness surrounds the place. On clear days one can see ridge after ridge after ridge as they proceed from green to blue to vanish in a faint hazy-grey at the very limit of vision. There seems to be no end to these mountains, no end to the hollows and shallow, tree-cloaked rivers.

Here one encounters the Eastern Divide. The tiny, unnamed creek running through the family homestead finally meets the orange slash of Raccoon Creek, which, joined by other creeks named and nameless, reaches a tributary of the Monongahela to run north, through valleys crowded with mills and iron foundries, toward Pittsburgh, its waters feeding the Ohio, which itself feeds the Mississippi as it drains the heartland of America into the warm and salty embrace of the Gulf of Mexico. Yet, scant miles away, other mountain brooks that, in their dark exuberance, look and sound exactly like mine, skip down to the North Branch of the Potomac, and hurry past Harpers Ferry to meet the sea at Chesapeake Bay.

Wedding Journey

for Gilda Mekler

White oaks
     stunted by weak mountain soil
flank the Appalachian Trail
where it starts down into this opening valley.

At lookout rocks
rain-heavy clouds push up grey

push up over
          and on east —
clouds
     like giant mammals
moisture thick
on flat green leaves,
our arms and faces.

We begin a life together
where the world slips from mist.
Through breaks in the weather
the Shenandoah is a silver dancer
     on an old sea bed

— from limestone ridge,
curling wash of minerals

rolling to the Chesapeake.

Culpeper, Winchester, Harpers Ferry, Frederick —
the towns and villages of my youthful trips to
cousins, aunts and uncles — stand sharp in my
rememberings. The sultry Shenandoah and
Stonewall Jackson's futile campaigns, buckwheat
cakes and farmers' sausage, white clapboard
houses and country churches, their silent
congregations stiff as corn stalks in the sun's heat

Six generations of Deahls spread across the land.
Almost all supporters of Jeffersonian democracy in
its day, and of the Union cause during the War
Between the States. They were, by and large, a
backwoods clan, preferring mountain wilderness
or the small town to life in large cities. Even today,
it's remarkable how very few of my relatives live in
the spreading metropoles that hold most of the
nation's population.

It was my father who left Preston County to live
in the big city. I was, therefore, quite unusual;
Deahls do not tend to grow up in places like
Pittsburgh. Were I a true representative of my
people, I'd have been raised in Kingwood, West
Virginia, home of the autumn Buckwheat Festival
and its annual harvest parade of tractor-pulled
floats and marching bands, led by beautiful Queen
Ceres and her royal consort, King Buckwheat.

Blue Ridge

XXXVI

  Heavy mountain cattle
and an airplane's shadow
     swift through goldenrod.

XXXVII

  Steep Blue Ridge pasture —
call of an unseen rooster
     returns to still grass.

XXXIX

Lip of the scree —
dragonfly rises out

one thousand feet of air.

XXXVIII

All day the gelding
drew plough through tight brown soil:
   site of the Union dead.

LXIX

      Sixth day of our wedding journey,
we cross this summer valley
              where Jackson's men once marched.

XL

      Shenandoah rain,
when clouds storm Hawksbill Gap;
           noisy buntings vanish.

XLI

Right out of grey rock
        this stand of chestnut oak
                encircles the rain.

XLII

      The storm now past:
           a bright pine grosbeak
solid rush of river.

There is something that attracts me strongly to locations where geography abruptly changes. This could be a result of being raised in Pittsburgh, the only truly important Eastern city west of the Appalachian Mountains, the only one whose rivers flow toward the Mississippi instead of the various bays and harbours of the eastern seaboard. If you leave the Golden Triangle and drive west for just one hour along U.S. 22 you're suddenly (and solidly) in the Midwest.

One can clearly see this in contemporary poetry. Gerald Stern (born in Pittsburgh, 1925) is an Eastern poet through and through. James Wright (Martins Ferry, 1927) is clearly a Midwestern poet. As to what makes "The Red Coal" an Eastern poem while "The Old WPA Swimming Pool in Martins Ferry, Ohio" can only be viewed as Midwestern in tone and sensibility . . . I can't say, but the shift interests me greatly. This is especially so because Stern and Wright — almost the same age — grew up not more than 65 miles apart. And Stern teaches at the University of Iowa, you can't get more Midwestern than Iowa; but no matter what, he remains Eastern, true to his roots.

This same fascination has always called me back to the Blue Ridge area. Here the Appalachian Trail winds between the Piedmont region and the mountains that form the almost impenetrable highlands of West Virginia and central Pennsylvania. Here silence, broken only by the odd squirrel or rummaging coon, cloaks river birch and the fugitive pawpaw; here rhododendron purples the pale shadows cast by the gathering trees.

To the east, tired old plantations stretch gently

to the sea: tobacco and corn, as far as the inward wash of tidewater.

To the west, the languid, fertile valley of the Shenandoah River, then suddenly, before one is prepared for them, the Appalachian Mountains, Shenandoah Mountains, Allegheny Mountains, Cheat Mountain, and the spreading Appalachian Highlands, range upon range upon range, mist brimming river valleys until noon, clouds shrouding the crested hills and summits.

Hawksbill Gap

Wild grape trails over
brown almost vertical
striped rock

Spine of Blue Ridge/
        forty thousand years
        exposed

the cliff bright
                        in afternoon
                        sun

Millipede in gravel
hiss of cool wind from the gorge

And on our summer trips we never missed a Sunday service; my father made sure of that. We would, of course, seek out a Presbyterian church, if one were at hand. If not, any denomination would do, so long as it was properly solemn and Calvinistic.

So we went. Village to village, each with its country graveyard lying under a few stolid hardwoods, each with its war monument uplifted in memory of the glorious dead, so lost in their dark earth. For the South stretches like a woman, shy and comfortable, uncorseted on vacation days with schools shut and the children helter-skelter in the molasses-warm woods.

Deep within the shady heat we sought crawfish, painted turtles, kingsnakes the long days through. The boundless joy of catching a Blue Ridge salamander or an elusive chorus frog remains a thing of childhood — a joy that can never be replicated in adult life. As evening settled into valleys, we'd release our terror-numbed prisoners into their native thicket or creek, then home to supper, tureens steaming on fumed oak tables.

And the short, sweaty nights; the whole countryside lying under a dark, heavy blanket of air almost too thick to breathe. Even the stars had a hard time penetrating the humid, yet cloudless, skies. So little rain; the days hazy, the nights black and hot, without wind. With morning, insects and birds would come alive in the white oven of the August sun.

Today, little has changed. Along winding roads the corn stands resolute and dry, dust covered leaves rustling to a thin breeze, the silk parched the color of broom straw. Men move among the fields. Farm women bend to tend kitchen gardens, laundry barely moving on the strung lines.

Drought

Brittle mountain pasture.
A maple with ten trunks
solitary/
                    overlooking
floodplain of the Potomac.

All afternoon a blister of haze,
insects along barbed wire
        tall with wild grass.
Red cows appear and disappear
in the sun's furnace.

Miles downstream
Harpers Ferry is a woman
in a pale blue dress.
The Shenandoah rises
heavy out of the southland.

On the narrow road out of town
revivalists pack the Baptist hall.
Reeds filled with
        an upright piano's song
and this line of solid trees
steadfast under a cloudless sky.

I have always been taken by the innocence, the
childlike innocence of small-town America. There
was a knack, if that's the correct word, of not
knowing the evils of this world. One certainly
knew the evils of Satan; daily Bible readings saw to
that. But the evils of day-to-day life, unless

sufficiently generalized, were simply not considered. Somehow television, newspapers, *Time* and *Newsweek*, mass communications failed to penetrate rural America as they had penetrated the urban centers when I was a teenager.

This innocence was attractive (or seductive) in a way that's hard to understand on any but the most emotional level. These folk did not ignore evil; they were too honest for that. They just didn't seem to see it. For them, evil was externalized, was out there, not in the hearts of modern Americans. They were, and in fact still are, good people who, sadly, do no good outside their restricted circle of family, friends, and church because they fail to see any need for larger deeds. They have become part of the problem without knowing there is a problem.

I remember riding with Terry Barker through western Pennsylvania, the river valleys lined with farms, all but the very steepest hills crested thick with hardwoods spotted here and there with the deeper greens of hemlock and pine. "Americans are children", he said . . . or did he say "Yanks"? No matter; I got his point.

This quality of decent innocence is often found in the Deahl family. Although educated, my kin tend to lack the sophistication of a truly urban people. But I grew up in Pittsburgh in a home in which newspapers were studied, television newscasts followed with care, and trips to the museum, art gallery, symphony, conservatory, and planetarium commonplace. I knew (or with that grand wisdom usually given to the young, thought I knew) what was happening in the world around me.

This is not to say that no one in my family took a keen interest in the world at large or in the spiritual and moral issues of the day. Thanks to the military, my uncle and aunt, Brigadier General & Mrs. Orman Charles, had lived all over the world (Asia, Africa, Europe, Oceana), and they understood much more than I did about most things. Even I was able, despite my grand wisdom, to recognize that.

Nonetheless, there is this *niceness* to many of my relatives that is not often associated with big city residents. In those days, one could simply not know about Harlem and Malcolm X in Tunnelton, West Virginia; such ignorance was unthinkable in New York, Los Angeles, or even Pittsburgh. I found this quality to be at once charming and — to be completely honest — intensely infuriating. With all the righteous fervour of the immature, I saw this as willed ignorance, as not wanting to know.

It must be that as urban Americans grow to adulthood they are hardened in ways quite different from the ways in which their more agrarian fellow citizens are hardened. While some might draw comfort from the idea that evil is restricted to monsters like Hitler or Stalin, to my mind, the evil that spawned World War II was an evil residing within human nature itself. It lives here, in each of us, as well as in whatever Hell may exist "out there".

Still, many city dwellers are taken by surprise by events they should have anticipated. The deindustrialization in the North is a case close to my heart. When I worked at United States Steel it was clear to me that the steel industry was inefficient. It seemed that only the needs of the War in Vietnam kept things running. Very little capital investment was taking place; mills were falling to pieces.

Yet even I was shocked by the speed at which the Smoke Stack North became the Rust Bucket North. Like an overworked Midwestern farm in the dusty thirties, the mills and factories blew away . . . so little had been put in for so long that collapse became almost inevitable. Many involved in industry — both management and labour — failed to see this coming. One day the mills closed forever; they were simply gone. Whole communities were ruined, their guts wrenched out.

There was anger, sure; but what could people do? For five generations, profits had been pulled out of the area; vast fortunes (Carnegie, Mellon, Frick, Laughlin) were made. And some of those profits had always returned in the form of new investment. Then fresh investment stopped; money left Pittsburgh, never to return. The people left behind, poor and often broken in spirit, could do nothing.

It's hard to say just when reinvestment dried up and the wealth started draining away, and it doesn't matter now. By the time I left Pittsburgh in 1970, this change was already in process.

Three Views of a River Town

I

along the Monongahela
homes of unemployed steelworkers

lean into dry slopes
row upon row

bright afternoon
light

II

not a barge
breaks the evening river

a pigeon —
an abandoned mill

the same space
across the water

III

darkness

over trees
and cracked yellow-brick buildings

soaring flame
of coke oven gas

silent   windy   night

McKeesport Coda

never again
     will steel be made at this place

sumac and black cherry
spring up

sumac
               black cherry
dusty millyard

Visiting my homeland during the years since I left,
I pass through an increasingly barren place lit, if it
is lit at all, by a dull light spilling down the
hungering streets. Old tugs list; a scatter of lilies
weeps where the river used to surge each spring, to
be measured by worried men until, all danger
passed, the level began to drop and the redbrick
factory stood safe for another year. And those
orchids I could never find in childhood — lady's-
slipper, ladies'-tresses, moccasin-flower, adder's-
mouth, snake-mouth, crested and fringed —
continue their occult lives by nameless runs or
deep, unvisited thickets. Surely the saprophytic
coralroot could thrive amid such decay, but its
leafless stalks remain forever hidden in these
brown, brown woods.

   My old school is gone; the shops are closed. Like
all boys I loved to play at construction sites,
turning bulldozers into battle tanks while
foundations became forts along some fierce and

remote frontier. And yet buildings I remember watching as their skeletons climbed the silver air have been demolished to be replaced by other, newer structures already falling into disuse. Before the 1960s, no one would have thought change on this scale possible. But then, no one would have thought the '60s possible. And who dares call this progress?

Still, there are other changes, social and human in nature, that run far deeper than the merely material and economic changes that seem to be of such keen and pressing concern.

We who grew up in the wake of the war have been reluctantly dragged into a delayed maturity, and the great sorrow is that it has not arrived soon enough. For most there was little or no time to re-establish ties to our roots and to our families. The generation that suffered through the Depression, World War II, the death camps, and the horrors associated with the dawning of the nuclear age — the generation that bore and raised us — is rapidly passing away. For many, myself among them, there was no opportunity to discover that those affections, deep and true, were still present until it was too late. Parents, grandparents, aunts and uncles were gone; there was no one to go home to.

On the Death of an Aged Aunt

for Wilma Deahl   (1910 - 1990)

The winter wind
On a branch outside the window
A single apple.

Against the springhouse
Stalks of frozen wildflowers
Scrape white stone.

Standing in your kitchen
How quickly the darkness comes
As autumn closes.

Unpruned since you left
That yellow rose twists around
The hollow wind.

The garden reclaimed!
Under the roof of the old barn
Swallow nests.

Interview

Comments largely taken from the June, 1992 interview conducted by David Allen Greene.

On the Deahl home at Hiorra, Preston County, West Virginia

It was, and in many ways still is, the nicest house in that neighborhood: the biggest house. For example, it's a full two stories; then there are all the outbuildings — springhouse, laundry, blacksmith shop, smokehouse, woodshed, barn. This is befitting one of the leading families in the community. My grandfather Ulysses built the home; he was a big wheel in the local coal mine. He worked underground and, of course, did suffer from black-lung; but Ulysses came to be more of a supervisor of coal miners than a miner himself.

Now, my uncles and my father worked in the mine too, to one degree or another. But the Deahl family was able to own its own home as opposed to having to live in one of the company houses. The home has a big, formal dining room as well as a parlor with a pot-bellied iron stove and a pump organ. There's a central stairway to the second floor that leads to a hall with bedrooms to the right and left.

As a general rule the house is dark inside. Because the land rises up so steeply around the house, and because of the encroachment of the forest, it is very shadowy and dark.

On Ulysses Grant Deahl (1868 - 1951)

Although I have one or two vivid memories of
Ulysses Deahl, he died when I was young and I did
not know him all that well. I will say, however, that
my grandfather seemed to be the typical West
Virginian — a rugged individual. The Deahls are a
very taciturn group; they never show emotion and
they do not have a lot to say about themselves. After
all, they've been living in the Appalachian Mountains
— deep in the narrow hollows or way back in the
highlands — for six generations. Ulysses was perhaps
typical of this mountain breed.

It is important to remember that these old coal
camps were isolated. They bred an insular,
independent people. Self-reliance might have been
Emerson's great ideal, but you find it all over West
Virginia. Conditions were rough; it was good to have
a certain type of personality.

On Henry Vance Deahl (1904 - 1993)

My father grew up at Hiorra and, although I had a
rather distant relationship with him, I have always
felt at home when visiting the old homestead. I was
adopted. Both the Deahls and my mother's people,
the Daubers, are of German-American stock. [In fact,
my adoptive family is German on all four sides: Deahl
(Diehl in Germany), Cale (Kahl in Germany), Dauber,
and Muller.] Perhaps because I am a Celt by birth, my
temperament was a bit different. Even though I have
a great deal of affection for my relatives — they are,
after all, my family — I did not always fit in well with
the Deahls.

My father was a hard-headed, practical man. And
he was tough, physically and emotionally, in ways I
cannot be tough. He had no interest in the arts. We

seemed to have very little common ground and our relationship was strained and difficult.

With time I have grown to respect his toughness. He knew how he wanted to live his life and he lived it that way. He was a man of courage and convictions. Such people are not always easy to live with.

On social change
and my relationship to my family

Although I hate the term, the Baby Boom Generation, of which I am one of the older members, stands on one side of an unprecedented generation gap (yet another term I usually object to). This has affected my life and, I guess, the lives of most people my age.

The large-scale protest against the U.S. invasion of Vietnam, which started to capture the attention of the major media about 1967 or '68, seemed to unite other protest movements: civil rights, women's liberation, student rights, anti-poverty groups, and environmental activists. It was a time of Woodstock and the Summer of Love.

More importantly, it was a time when people from all economic classes and, significantly, from different racial and ethnic groups were drawn together. Don't forget, when I grew up in Forest Hills there were no Black people around. I never had any interaction with Blacks until I started to attend high school in Wilkinsburg, and my interaction there was very limited. So all these different people were suddenly drawn together into single-issue protest groups. They began to question authority.

Although actual change has been painfully slow, the spirit of challenge and rebirth was something I, and others like me, noticed. A generation gap was caused that, in one way or another, affected every citizen of the country. Things might not have seemed all that different, but they would never be the same.

These protest movements that began to gain force about the time I reached adulthood were extremely American. Although often referred to as the "counterculture", they were, and still are, part of a culture that worships Progress. That is, these social justice movements (as we call them now in the 1990s) are based on the notion that mankind is perfectible. With only a few exceptions, the leaders of my generation saw themselves as people who wanted to speed up a process that America had already set in motion; they simply wanted to reach their goals faster. I do not think that many of these activists viewed themselves as being anti-American, although their parents and government often did. One might say they were "Americans in a hurry", so much so that they became alienated from their families.

It was almost impossible, during the '60s and '70s, to understand the nature of the change that was required; I know I had neither the tools nor the experience. Now that we are middle-aged and, hopefully, somewhat more mature, it's a bit easier to see what's wrong with modernity. Sure, it made a good story: people and the media thought there was a *revolution* going on twenty-five years ago. They were wrong; the revolution (if there is to be one) will take place in the future, and it must be anti-American. By that I mean it must question Progress as well as authority. It must question the very Enlightenment concepts that support Americanism.

But perhaps things won't change much. Change — and here I'm speaking of real change — is hard; it puts one at risk. And it's nice to feel that our modern world simply needs improvement, a little fine tuning perhaps, to set matters straight. Maybe those painful questions concerning the assumptions that modernity is founded upon will not be asked in a clear and public way.

With maturity comes the understanding that very few things or people are all bad or all good. I try to go about my work in a slow and cooperative manner. The haste and aggressiveness, natural aggressiveness, of youth — and I had my share and then some — are better set aside. The world seems to move ever faster, ever more intensely. The arts of reflection and contemplation are as needed now as they ever were.

On poverty in West Virginia and Pittsburgh

West Virginia has been a sort of colony of the big industrial cities of the north, such as Pittsburgh. West Virginia is basically a place where resources come from; consequently, West Virginia's wealth was "exported" and was not kept within the state. The people were kept very poor and all the wealth ended up in the big northern cities.

One can see how wealthy people benefit their cities. In the days when the Mellon family lived in Pittsburgh and had a lot of involvement with Pittsburgh industries, there was a certain degree of prosperity in the area. Today, the Mellon family has largely cleared out — things that were Mellon companies like Gulf Oil are no longer Mellon companies, and there are hardly any Mellons involved with the running of Mellon Bank. In fact, the Mellons have moved themselves, as well as their capital, out of Pittsburgh. Very, very few, and none that I know of with the big money, remain. But when the Mellons were in Pittsburgh, they would draw wealth from other parts of the country. This wealth would be concentrated in Pittsburgh. Now that the Mellons have left town so has everything else.

On the death of the Pittsburgh steel mills

With industrial production, large groups of people are concentrated in one industry, working in one plant, or one factory, or one steel mill. Those people often live in a clearly defined community. For example, look at all the people living in the South Side of Pittsburgh who used to work at the big Jones and Laughlin mill. They see themselves as having common interests and a common bond. Consequently, there was a lot of community spirit during strikes or lock-outs, when people who had fallen on hard times were supported by their neighbours.

When that is gone, when the basis of that feeling of comradeship or brotherhood is gone, something really attractive leaves that community. Workers and their families are just left on their own without any sense of belonging to anything. That is the great loss that the destruction of the steel mills has brought about in the Pittsburgh area.

I grew up in a working-class district and attended working-class schools. It is easy — too easy — to romanticize working people and their culture. But it is also too easy to see blue-collar life as mean and depressing. The fact is that the mills were the lifeblood of a great many Pittsburgh-area communities and now they are gone.

When the mill closes it is as if the community and its people have no reason to exist. Welfare is not the same as a job; unlike working in the mill, welfare is mean and depressing. These people are being destroyed.

On the need to write poetry

In January of 1964 I decided to become a poet. I had recently read Allen Ginsberg's "HOWL" and a poem by an obscure poet named Lesley Irish. Both of those poets spoke to me in a way that allowed me to see that poetry was something that could not only speak to the issues and concerns of one's own life, but could operate as a tool to allow the poet to discover an organizing principle outside of day-to-day human life. That is, poetry could support one in the efforts of living one's life.

So in the middle of my final year of high school, I decided that I needed poetry in my life; I needed to read it and I needed to write it. If I could find a way to speak to people as Ginsberg or Sandburg spoke to me . . . that would be something worth working for.

On early influences

The two poets whose work most influenced me when I was just starting out in poetry were Carl Sandburg and Allen Ginsberg. As I recall, the first volumes of adult poetry I read after committing myself to poetry were *HOWL and Other Poems* (by Ginsberg) and *Honey and Salt* (by Sandburg). Although it was Ginsberg who got me hooked on poetry, his influence did not last long. Sandburg, on the other hand, stuck with me, or I stuck with him. He taught me what poetry could be.

Later on I was strongly influenced by Dylan Thomas, Gary Snyder, Denise Levertov, and, later still, by Robert Bly and Robert Duncan. (Today there are several poets whose new books I buy on sight: Levertov, Bly, W.S. Merwin, Mark Strand, Phyllis Webb, Seamus Heaney.) For the first half-dozen years

I wrote poems that were highly derivative; there is no other way to learn the craft. I never developed my own voice, my own vision, until I moved to Canada in 1970.

Dylan Thomas gets to the heart of the basic human experiences in the physical life that we live. I like that. He gets down to the essential elements of sex, reproduction, and death. Because of this, he remains one of our greatest erotic poets. "A Winter's Tale" is just marvellous.

On Carl Sandburg

In my very early days my biggest influence was Carl Sandburg, who still remains a strong influence in my life and work. Sandburg has this great faith in humanity, a faith that there's something really decent and good in human nature and the human personality, while nonetheless recognizing all the evil that people do and are capable of doing. That's his great strength. His great weakness is his belief in the whole enterprise of America. Sandburg didn't understand that Americanism works against anything that's good or decent in human nature.

He thought that people — the people — would eventually overcome America and redeem the country. He thought that this hideous legacy of exploitation and violence and oppression — that is really American history — could be redeemed and that people would establish some sort of just society.

To be fair, it is easy to think this. People want to think this. There is something truly attractive about such optimism. It is what I always loved in Emerson, who had a strong influence on my thought when I was a high school student. Sandburg was still alive and writing when I started out and I saw him as a man who was putting Emerson's ideas into practice in the twentieth century.

On Walt Whitman and American gnosticism

I have never liked Whitman's writing. It's very wordy, very discursive and overelaborated. He does, of course, have a few good pieces such as "When Lilacs Last in the Dooryard Bloomed", but even that is overwritten.

Whitman's poetry lacks any sense of humility, any sense that man has a place within the universe as opposed to the responsibility of running the universe. Walt Whitman is basically involved in becoming God. Thus, he becomes the great poet of the American Empire.

What is important with Whitman is that, in terms of the culture of Modernity, he was the first Modern poet in the world. He had a belief in the common man, as opposed to an elite. He also had a strong belief in man redeeming himself, rather than man being redeemed through the grace of God. In many ways, what twentieth century people have come to believe about themselves can be found in Whitman. He was the first poet to say these things.

Whitman and those like him — people like Hart Crane, for example, or Carl Sandburg, who is very similar to Whitman in many respects — believe that, although there may have been a fall of man, a fall from grace, people are not redeemed through some supernatural event like the second coming of Christ, but through human effort. The poet who understands that greatly is Robert Duncan, who was a disciple of Walt Whitman. According to the Christian religion, Christ was sent to Earth to die for the sins of mankind. This was the first coming. Then there is the notion that there'll be a second coming, and at this time history will end and humanity will be redeemed. Robert Duncan's understanding is that the second coming of Christ is not a second coming of someone sent down from Heaven; the American people are to become so Christ-like that they will redeem the human race.

And there is something quite attractive about this dilation of the ego. There is a certain attraction to American gnosticism, and I understand that. Who would not want to become god-like . . . to transcend human error? While gnosticism is spiritually destructive, there is an attraction to the idea of being among the god-like elect.

On Gary Snyder

One person to whom my work has been akin is Gary Snyder. His collection *The Back Country* was extremely important in the development of my own poetry. I started to read Snyder while I was a student at West Virginia Wesleyan College. Snyder actually left the United States and lived in Japan for several years; that impressed me. He has achieved absolutely marvellous things in his own poetry. I often use his work as a standard against which I measure mine.

The problem with Snyder's later work is he moved back to the United States thinking that somehow he had risen above it, or had gotten beyond it, or was immune to it. When Gary Snyder got to be really famous as an American poet around 1970 — *The Back Country* had been published in '68 — he became sort of a guru for a whole generation, for my generation, in fact. And he began believing too much in himself and in a spiritual revival of America that was not possible within the terms of America itself.

What happened was he moved outside the United States, produced a lot of amazing work, then moved back home and became a bit corrupted by the very Americanism he had been so critical of before. But the Gary Snyder of the 1960s is a poet with whom I feel a great affinity.

On great poetry and poets

What's important is that a poet has a vision and articulates that vision well. Milton Acorn used to teach that to write a great poem one had to start with a great thought. The rest was content finding its form.

Take T.S. Eliot. What makes Eliot a great poet is he believed in that High-Tory, Church-of-England ideal, and he articulated it very well. Now you don't have to believe in Toryism to be inspired by Eliot; I find myself being inspired by Eliot and I'm no Tory.

What makes a great poet ultimately is the ability to think and write well. Therefore, although I disagree with almost all of what Robert Duncan has to say, my belief is that Duncan is the high point of Modernist, English-language poetry. All those poets, Ezra Pound, T.S. Eliot, Walt Whitman, William Carlos Williams, Charles Olson, Marianne Moore, were leading up to the production of a Robert Duncan. So I would rate him as one of the great poets of our time. Indeed, I think Duncan is the most significant English-language poet of our century. He writes so well!

Another great Modernist poet is Denise Levertov. I greatly admire her work although I don't subscribe to Christianity. But that does not really matter; what I love in her work is her pure ability to write. And yes, I even read and reread her Christian poems.

This is important. I think very few readers, if they were judging on the basis of content alone, could like Levertov and Duncan at the same time, one being a Christian and the other being a representative of the Anti-Christ. My point is that readers do not have to be into gnosticism or Christianity to appreciate their books.

What I like about Denise Levertov is that she is very brief, very succinct in her poetry, very much involved in an economy of language. Robert Duncan, on the other hand, is like Whitman and Allen Ginsberg in that he's very full of his own language. You can spend a whole lifetime reading Levertov and Duncan and you will learn a lot about how to make great poetry. I discover something new every time I read Levertov and Duncan, and I read their poetry often.

One of the important things about Duncan is that right now there's a mass culture in the world which is largely American. This is no mistake because the goal of the United States is to make everyone into an American. Now whether you like the concept of the Americanization of our planet or not, it is important to know what it's about. If you read Robert Duncan (his "A Poem Beginning With A Line By Pindar", for example) you will know what Americanism is about at its highest spiritual level.

On the infinite

When one is young it's very easy to believe in this life, and in the importance of this life. It's easy to embrace living in a very passionate way. But ultimately I think people come to realize that this life passes away and that the things of this life pass away. Your parents pass away, a place like Hiorra passes away; all this is very temporary. The thing I'm struck by now is how brief — how fleeting life is, and how long eternity is.

There's an order in the universe, outside of our day-to-day existence here, that we might become aware of if we are thoughtful and reflective. Things here are transitory, but the infinite is always there. Nonetheless, we do live in a fleeting world and, consequently, there are feelings of sorrow, feelings of regret or melancholy. Even in our happiest moments we realize that this life is very temporary.

There is a separation. There is an awareness of a gulf between (if you want to use Christian terms) the order of Heaven, where things are permanent and eternal, and our world, which is fallen and passing. An appreciation of that gulf leads quite naturally to feelings of sorrow. The recognition of this separation — the Tao that can be known / the Tao that cannot be known — is central to Taoist thought.

On loss

I don't think you can get away from the topic of loss if you come out of mid-century American culture. For one thing, the men who founded the United States two hundred years ago had been, to one degree or another, Christians. It does not matter that the country they founded is no longer a Christian country, they had that whole theological structure at the start. In the case of the United States this would be the New Jerusalem, where mankind is redeemed. This is, of course, an anti-Christian message.

Biblical teaching has it that God will, at the end of time, bring about the apocalypse. This is the end of history and of life here in this realm. At that point the worthy are saved and the unworthy are condemned. But, in the myth of America it is the American people who build up a nation which becomes the New Jerusalem. Thus, mankind is saved by the American people, who first save themselves and then save the rest of the world. The whole American enterprise is about the self-redemption of man.

Now let's say you reject Americanism. Maybe you want to follow the teachings of Christ, or maybe you want to follow Plato, or the teachings of Taoism. In each case you have to say that man cannot save himself. That is, if people have a soul that requires saving, it's not they themselves who can save it. From this understanding of the human condition flows a sense of loss. We are fallen; we are flawed. We are not angels; we are not Christs. We cannot redeem ourselves. (Yet how we long for forgiveness!)

And you have to experience that loss *as a loss* in order to gain something else. You might gain a belief in God or you might gain a belief in Natural Law. You might gain a belief in an order that exists outside of man or you might gain a belief in something that is greater than your own personal ego. But it is necessary that you experience the loss that lies at the heart of the human condition before you can move on to a deeper understanding.

On pessimism

If you believe a pessimist is one who is not enthusiastic about man in the here-and-now, then I'm a pessimist. I don't think that the human enterprise on Earth is going very well at the moment. But if one talks about optimism or pessimism in terms of things that are ultimate — what in Taoism would be called "the infinite" or in Christianity would be called "the eternal" — then I am optimistic. But our own particular little piece of the universe, our own particular piece of human history, is certainly not anything to get overjoyed about.

One of the beautiful things about the natural world is that it is out of control. By that I mean that it is beyond human control. The natural world obeys natural laws, it obeys the order that lies behind the universe. Modern man wants to believe that through science he can control nature and the world, can bend reality to his will. Now, people may rebel against the order of the universe, but they cannot get the rest of creation to go along. And that's a beautiful thing.

On the Presbyterian Church

I was raised in the Forest Hills Presbyterian Church. My quarrel with the church is the teaching that God's providence is understandable — is revealed — within human history. That is, if you study human history you will come to understand God's will.

Modern people, Marxists as well as Capitalists, believe in history. They think of history as holding the great truths of the universe, and this makes man the focus of human study. Clearly, if one is going to be a Christian, the focus of human study should be the teachings of Christ, not some record of merely human events.

The problem faced by the church is that there is an order to the universe that is out there, that's beyond man and human things. This order is prior to the start of history; and being eternal (or infinite), it will carry on beyond the end of history. The proper subject of human worship, or human speculation, or human meditation is that which is out there. But Modern people don't want to believe this. They don't want to believe that there is anything beyond man or against which man can be measured.

When a nation sets out to construct Heaven on Earth, it is hard to promote humility and the worship of God. But then, if the elect can understand providence, can the church prevent the ascent of man to his "proper" place in the City on the Hill?

On my leaving Pittsburgh

I left Pittsburgh in the spring of 1970 when I was twenty-four years old. Perhaps because I entered manhood during the 1960s, I had initially intended to relocate to San Francisco. It was a fellow Pittsburgher, Tony Sullivan, who talked me into immigrating to Canada — going up country, as it was known then. Tony worked with me at The Book Stall, in those days the finest privately owned bookshop in the Steel City. Tony had been reading the works of one Edward George Bulwer, first Baron Lytton of Knebworth (1803-1873), better known as Edward Bulwer-Lytton. Bulwer-Lytton and other Golden Dawn authors convinced Tony that Canada was indeed the future home of the "coming race". Sullivan was a romantic and on an almost daily basis I heard of the wonders of Canada, of its great and shining future.

At the same time I was becoming ever more frustrated with my political work. Like many of my generation, I'd first been politicized by the Cuban missile crisis during the autumn of 1962. Kennedy's New Frontier was shown to be just the same old American imperialism. I started to read the radical journal *The Minority of One* and, by the time I met Tony, I'd been involved, to one degree or another, with Black Civil Rights, the Grape Boycott, and the mass opposition to the War in Vietnam. Although I was never involved to the extent that poets like Robert Bly and Denise Levertov were, I had been part of the Resistance right up until I left the country.

None of these reform movements seemed to me to be going anywhere. The Civil Rights movement was met with ever more violent outbursts of government supported racism and the murder of Martin Luther King, Jr. Violence and racism also formed the establishment's response to the farm workers' drive for union recognition and decent working conditions. And as for the war, when over 300,000 anti-war protesters marched on Washington in November 1969, the U.S. response was to invade Kampuchea less than six months later.

It's fair to say that I was fed up with the United States when I drove my pick-up truck to Ottawa, where my first wife and I had found a rented room in the Sandy Hill area. I applied for permanent admission to Canada on June 8, 1970, at the height of the war in Kampuchea. It seemed like a damned good time to leave the U.S.A.

(I should note that my political work, such as it was, continued after my move to Canada. I remained active in the Grape Boycott, for example. And I later became a minor organizer with the disarmament movement.)

In 1970 I had few reasons to be in Canada except that it was not the United States. Now, twenty-two years later, I can say that I'm most attracted to Canada because of its tradition of Natural Law philosophy. Canada as we know it today was established by the United Empire Loyalists — Americans who opposed the Revolutionary War. These refugees started arriving in 1775 and well over 40,000 had settled in Ontario, New Brunswick, and Nova Scotia by 1784. [In fact, as I edit this interview during the summer of 1993, celebrations are going on to mark the 200th anniversary of the opening of the London District to settlement by U.E. Loyalists and other English-speaking people.]

The Loyalists came here because they wanted what I have always wanted: peace, order, and good government. I must add that belief in Natural Law (the concept of an order in the universe that is beyond man) as a founding principle for human society no longer exists in any shape or form; Canada is now much too Modern for that. Nevertheless, the watchwords of peace, order, and good government still enjoy a certain currency here.

One benefit of living in Canada is that I've been put in touch with cultural traditions that are non-American and non-Modern. When one lives in the States, one must maintain a relationship with the whole American enterprise. One is either part of it, participating in and supporting it; or, as I was in the 1960s, opposed to it and struggling to overthrow it. It's extremely hard — impossible really — to get free of the establishment and its concerns unless one gets free of the U.S. by moving to another country.

When I was in the U.S. I had trouble seeing anything but America. The U.S. is, after all, the first and greatest Modern nation in the world; there's tremendous pressure to believe that the only things that matter are things that have happened since the Declaration of Independence in 1776. For Americans the break with the past was severe; history, religion, and philosophy all start with the Enlightenment, with the spiritual and political revolutions it spawned.

Canada, by contrast, has tended to maintain its connection to older traditions. Although French settlement dates back almost four centuries — to 1608 when Samuel de Champlain founded Quebec —

many contemporary French-speaking Canadians still like to trace their roots back to Bourbon France. To a much greater degree many English-speaking people (those of British North American stock as well as those who want to be) view themselves as English. (Except for the Scots, that is!) Then there are the new Canadians from eastern and southern Europe as well as from the Orient, Latin America, Africa, and the Caribbean. Due in part to the government's emphasis on multiculturalism, these people also prize their non-American roots.

Looked at in terms of poetry, American literature starts with Anne Bradstreet and Edward Taylor. Canadian literature starts, quite properly, with Chaucer. Since moving north, I too have learned to look beyond the Revolution.

In any event, I had lived in Canada for a dozen years before I came to write most of the poems in *Under the Watchful Eye*. After Gilda and I were married, we journeyed to my family seat, Hiorra, and the Blue Ridge country for our honeymoon. By this time I had a better idea why I did not like the American enterprise. I also had a better idea of what it was about my homeland and its people that I did find handsome. America is neither completely bad nor completely good. To see it as one or the other (as I used to) is to not see it at all. I had come to some important decisions about America by the spring of 1982. These new understandings have informed my poetry; the pieces collected earlier in this book would have been different had I not left my homeland at the age of twenty-four.

Although I had been writing and publishing poetry for a few years prior to my move north, I managed to write only three worthwhile pieces during the 1960s; the rest was juvenilia. Thus, one must take Canada and the experience of immigration into consideration when evaluating my work. If I am read as an American poet, I'm an American poet who has lived outside the U.S. for his entire career; if I am read as a Canadian poet, I'm a Canadian who came to this country as an adult, his personality to a large degree already formed.

But times change. In this age of the New World Order, I find myself in an interesting position. The economic and cultural nationalism I encountered in Canada as a young man is being replaced by an embracing of all things American and a continentalist fervor that was unthinkable when my eldest daughter was born in the autumn of 1972. For better or worse (and I'd say worse) Canadians are learning to view themselves as Americans of the U.S. variety.

It seems I moved to Canada to escape Americanism only to find that many Canadians wanted, more than anything else, to become Americans. Continentalism grants them the chance.

ૐ

About the Author

James Deahl was born in Pittsburgh (USA) in 1945. His mother's family is from the Laurel Highlands coal mining district of Pennsylvania and his father's family is from the Allegheny Mountains region of West Virginia. He visited these areas often while growing up.

He moved to Canada in 1970 and has lived in many Ontario cities and villages: Ottawa, Almonte, Sudbury, Wanup, Toronto, and London. Currently he lives in Hamilton with his wife, the artist Gilda Mekler, and their daughters, Simone and Shona. His eldest daughter, Sarah, lives and works in Toronto.

Deahl serves as President of the Canadian Poetry Association and is a partner in Mekler & Deahl, Publishers.

James Deahl is available for poetry readings and lectures through
The League of Canadian Poets,
54 Wolseley Street, 3rd floor,
Toronto, Ontario M5T 1A5
Phone: (416) 504-1657; fax (416) 947-0159.

See and hear what you just read ...

If you would like to hear the nuances of the poet's voice and to experience visually the multi-layered environment in which these poems are grounded, order the related video and tape.

Under The Watchful Eye began as a video inspired by a selection of James Deahl's poetry, most written in West Virginia and Virginia in 1982 on the poet's honeymoon. This book was produced as a companion; an audiocassette pairs the poet's voice with the evocative bluegrass of D.C. Fitzgerald.

The video is an engrossing exploration of several of the threads that run through James Deahl's poetry. It follows his journey into the land of his boyhood, probing subjects that matter to him: coal mining, beehive coke ovens, the Blue Ridge Mountains, the American Civil War, and the death of the steel industry in Pittsburgh. Deahl's poetry is presented in a powerful integration with music and visuals that capture the haunting beauty of the Appalachian mountains and of the often dark human history they held. Other voices are also heard: writers, artists, scholars, coal miners and steelworkers.

The original music written by singer/guitarist D.C. Fitzgerald for the video was so good that it cried out for a soundtrack recording. *Poetry and Music From Under the Watchful Eye* captures James Deahl's voice reading the ten poems in this book, along with the compelling tunes in the video and another 30 minutes of D.C.'s music available nowhere else. D.C. is well respected for his work in the folk and blues traditions. He has recorded solo and with bands (Common Threads and DC), and has performed at clubs and festivals throughout the United States for the past quarter-century.

Price and order information:

(Prices include shipping, handling, and applicable taxes)

Under the Watchful Eye (the video)
Written and produced by David A. Greene. Silver Falls Video:
North Huntingdon, PA. 60 min., Hi-fi stereo, VHS. SF-93-501.

Price:	US:	$23.45
	Canada:	$34.00
	New Brunswick (includes PST):	$37.74

Poetry and Music from Under the Watchful Eye (tape)
Poetry by James Deahl; Music by D.C. Fitzgerald. Broken Jaw
Press: Fredericton, NB. 60-min. audiotape. ISBN 0-921411-32-4

Price:	US:	$10.45
	Canada:	$15.00
	New Brunswick (includes PST)	$16.50

Under The Watchful Eye: Poetry and Discourse (book)
James Deahl. Trade paperback, 64 pp. Broken Jaw Press:
Fredericton, NB. ISBN 0-921411 30-8.

| **Price:** | US: | $10.45 |
| | Canada: | $15.00 |

Under The Watchful Eye: Book and Video Set
James Deahl; David A. Greene. Broken Jaw Press: Fredericton,
NB. ISBN 0-921411-31-6

Price:	US:	$30.50
	Canada:	$43.00
	New Brunswick (includes PST)	$45.94

To Order:

In the US: **Silver Falls Video Productions**
283 Carpenter Lane
North Huntingdon, PA 15642-1239 USA

In Canada: **Broken Jaw Press/M•A•P Productions**
Box 596, Stn, A,
Fredericton NB E3B 5A6 Canada

The audiotape may also be ordered by calling
1-800-JOE-RADIO (1-800-563-7234)

Other Items of Interest

Broken Jaw Chapbooks

Salvador. A.J. Perry. 0-921411-12-X
Drawings by Poet. Beth Jankola. 0-921411-13-8
Hawthorn. Arthur Bull; Ruth Bull (illustrator). 0-921411-24-3
poems from the blue horizon. rob mclennan. 0-921411-14-0

Broken Jaw Press

Chaste Wood. karl wendt. 0-921411-28-6
A Lad from Brantford & other essays. David Adams Richards.
0-921411-25-1
voir dire. pj flaming. 0-921411-26-X
Under The Watchful Eye: Poetry and Discourse. James Deahl.
0-921411-30-8
Under The Watchful Eye: Book & Video Set. James Deahl;
David A. Greene. 0-921411-31-6
Poetry and Music from Under the Watchful Eye. James Deahl;
D.C. Fitzgerald. (audio) 0-921411-32-4
Only the Salt. Doug Underhill. 0-921411-35-9

Maritimes Arts Projects Production

Ripples from the Phoenix. Diana Smith. 0-921411-29-4
Memories of Sandy Point, St. George's Bay, Newfoundland. Phyllis
Pieroway, Charles Warren Pieroway. 0-921411-33-2

New Muse Manuscript Award

An annual award for poets with no prior books published.
Manuscripts of 50–65 pages with a $15 entry fee accepted
before March 31 of each year. The winner of the New Muse
Award is announced in May and the award-winning book
published in autumn by Broken Jaw Press. The 1994 winner is
pj flaming for *voir dire*. Send SASE for full guidelines.

New Muse of Contempt

A semi-annual international magazine of mail art and literary
writings—poetry, visual poetry, essays, fiction and reviews—
edited and published since 1987 by Joe Blades.
ISSN 0840-4747 $7/year

To order, or for full catalogue, please write to:
Broken Jaw Press/M•A•P•Productions
Box 596 Stn A
Fredericton NB E3B 5A6   Canada